THE TRICK

Patrick Davidson Roberts was born in 1987 and grew up in Sunderland and Durham. He was editor of The Next Review magazine 2013-2017 and in 2019 he ran All My Teachers, the all-women reading series. In 2018 Vanguard Editions published *The Mains*, his debut collection, and his work has been published in *Ambit, The Dark Horse, Eyot, Magma, The Quince* and *The Rialto* as well as on *Wild Court,* and *The High Window,* for whom he also reviews. He lives and works in London.

Also by Patrick Davidson Roberts

The Mains   (Vanguard Editions, 2018)

There is a twist in Patrick Davidson Roberts' lines, between the compelling and compulsive voices, the grace of rhyme, the stubbed ends of stories, the bars and the stars. The twist is poetry.

— Alison Brackenbury

In beautifully-managed long lines across sixteen poems, Patrick Davidson Roberts has given us a picture of hell: local, personal, vividly and violently realised. You can open these poems up and walk about in them, with a growing, unnerving sense that they're places you've visited beforehand, between sleep and waking.

— John Clegg

Patrick Davidson Roberts gives us powerful, moving narratives of modern masculinity and strong whisky, double-crossing and cross-dressing. Smoking is a smokescreen to cover the scent of an affair; a boy 'tries on four masks in twelve seconds.' Pain – the 'white smile' of a scar – is balanced with wry and tender humour. These poems are subtle tricksters: just when you think you've stripped off every layer, another is revealed. Pick up *The Trick* and prepare to be beguiled.

— Yvonne Reddick

These are poems as 'below-table-communication', attuned to the rhythms of the vernacular, to the tricks played in what's said and what remains unspoken, thinking 'night thoughts'. There is a constant layering at play, in language – spotting the lyre in the liar – and in the art of covering up, which as often as not proves a means to mask further diversion. This is writing rich in nuance, voiced by narrators who have taken enough, but who bear their scars as proof of 'the healing of time'.

— Declan Ryan

for David Harsent

ISBN: 978-1-915760-14-2

Cover designed by Aaron Kent

Edited by Kit Ingram

Typeset by Aaron Kent

Broken Sleep Books Ltd
Rhydwen
Talgarreg
Ceredigion
SA44 4HB

Broken Sleep Books Ltd
Fair View
St Georges Road
Cornwall
PL26 7YH

Contents

I am no longer a participant: once more, I am an observer. To observe is not to not feel – in fact it is to put yourself at the mercy of feeling, like the child's warm skin meeting the cold air of midnight.

— *Rachel Cusk*

I don't like the fact that, nowadays, it feels like it's not permissible to leave something unresolved ... Some people live with their trauma for years. I'm not interested in rubbing people's faces in suffering ... But I don't like this lie that everybody gets over things that easily. Some people can't get over something major that's happened to them at all; why can't they have a movie too?

— *Kenneth Lonergan*

Aubade

Again with the early to waking, again with the week ahead dropping from me,
I navigated dawn, packed night thoughts and their kind away.
Jem came back into the room, naked as the open hinge, and sat on the side of
        the bed.
'You've got a few hours, you know, until work. We could always try.'
She patted the blank space between us, read the panic in me
and lowered herself to it all, her stomach flat across my spine.
Twisting until she was sealed along me,
she picked at the back of my hand with her teeth
until it untwisted, and she took it on, down to the sheet, out to the edge.

Trick to Get Out of the Wedding

You have to unfold the placename before you until its crease
slips the invitation back into the envelope, which will lift
the pen from paper and remove your name from their list.
Once this is done, raise the glass back to your mouth
and quietly let the claret slip from between your lips
into the cup, so the two of you don't argue on that evening.
Now hold your right palm over the tealight on the table
and once the black cracks and hisses, reason that
this is a hand you could not use to tilt her face to yours.
After this, walk carefully to the toilets past the dancefloor
and close the door behind you, which will shut the door
that he was going to fix that night the two of you gave him dinner.
Once inside the cubicle, recite the name on the toilet before you
that will take back all the words that you learnt at school
through the discomfort of its sound - remake girls unfamiliar.
When you get back to the table, try to ignore the speeches,
because as a kid you hated public places
and everyone is worried because the child is acting oddly.
To finish, leave before the dancing, and don't answer
when they ask whether you introduced them.
Step back into the warm dark. Split apart again.

Miracles

Not believing has a sickness, which is believing a little.

— *Antonio Porchia*

There are folk round here talking miracles.
You see them on the corner, eyes up at the streetlights,
and you hear them streets away
as they rant their prophecy, arms at speed and handsfree dangling.
What gets me is their certainty; really,
I'm after telling them to shut it, but only because the surety
of someone pronouncing God on the pavement
is taken away from madness for me because of how much they mean it.
I'm the kid in the camp under Sinai,
three-thou' back and asking me mam if the fella with the foreign wife
who did the plagues and then the sea and brought us to this place is legit,
or whether one morning we're packing up and away back to Goshen?
They all look mental, prophets, That's the trick, I suppose.
I can think of few things harder than being the one in those clothes.

The Mark

For years I'd mistaken her narcissism for a sure sign of the easily led.
It took separation to realise that to hate yourself to that certain degree,
while convinced that your own company is the best around,
brings home the horror of the marooned. Not even mirrors to torture you,
you are your own reproduction: the perfect copy that your mind
decided long ago to set you looking at alone.
This isn't to say that, years later, when meeting, I wasn't still set on proving
that before and after all else she must be an easy mark to the vengeful.
Carrying my tools in the same hands as alcohol – I am sometimes reluctant
to tell one from the other – I'm not a particularly subtle trickster,
and most who've spent any time with me know this.
They also know that my interest alters if I catch a speck of the unexpected
in someone I'd only thought to trick. I'd let someone with cash by the bundle
falling out of their bag get away, even shield them from the plays of others,
if they mentioned something new on Anne Sexton,
or could convince me as to why the Ninth is really the best of Beethoven.
That afternoon, mind, I'd other designs, and had really worked them out,
but after a few and some more cigarettes, I saw that I'd be moving on.
Not that I'd managed to get a sentence in: she talked for two hours,
casting a galactic orbit of interlinked detail to all that passed
around her as fixed, and laying out why this system was the only one worth
                    mentioning.
I'd thought that that would be enough to spur me on, to trick her out of something
and walk away with enough in my hand that she'd not feel the lack of til later.
But I caught myself on her second circuit. I mean, *living* like that? Wheeled in on
                    yourself
as the orbit rots and diminishes over the years, until the final plunge of the axis?
Hadn't she already taken enough?

The Trick

I hustle. Never been afraid to hustle.

— *Lisa Maffia*

The trick I developed years ago was that on my evening walk – a habit
that long preceded him but which the circumstances of our relationship
greatly enhanced the need for – I'd smoke at least two to each
can that I drank, reasoning that his insistence on my Listerine shot
once back in the flat was better than the alternative of him twigging the smell
of harder stuff and having to ask if it was really that bad?
Did I need that much to drink before we spent the evening together?

Scent not being water, though, nor a time machine nor a good night's sleep,
I'm pretty sure that after a while he realised me to be drunk,
but reasoned – as he once delicately, well kind of, put – that
I'm obviously one of those guys who gets a bit high from nicotine.
Granted, we both knew that I'd been smoking since eleven
and that I'm definitely not one of those guys, but I appreciated
his effort. It's why we parted so calmly – or was at least one of the reasons.

Six years on, and living with her, I ran into an obstacle:
does the trick work when your partner smokes too?
Not only a smoker but, like me then, partial to enough cocaine
that our senses of smell never existed, really, as part of that relationship.
We had only our eyes; fortunately we were open enough
with one another that I could drink that amount in front of her
and not worry. She already knew it was really that bad.

This openness was probably why I took the trick
to its logical extreme. Meeting up one Christmas Eve with her
for a heavy yank brunch in a Soho whiskey joint,
I'd smoked the best part of a packet earlier
having woken up, not for the first time, in the arms of someone else.
Alcohol being one thing, but a lover being another,
I set to the Benson and Hedges with a passion like few before.

I'd got to this place before her – Jackson and Rye, remember them –
and realised, seven cigarettes in, that the woman in question
didn't actually wear perfume. Which oddly made it worse:
could the trick dispel the scent of love (mine, not the absence of hers)?
No matter the acrid waste on my tongue, I felt my whole self
rinsed in the night before, the taste of that woman on me
and the scented weight of her conversation like tear gas or pepper-spray.

Hence the double Bloody Mary, hence the Jack and Ginger:
the slippery slope of the upgraded trick that was trying to cover
the smell of the cover and because living your life like this,
I'd discovered, is a fucking good reason to drink.
You'll have guessed that the old *food turned to ash in my mouth* thing
doesn't work, when you've basically washed in an ashtray
before getting to the table. After time, everything's ash.

Years later, when friends, she remarked fairly often
that 'You don't *really* smoke.'
And while I knew it was meant from her as a snipe
about me lacking the talk, and the walk, and anyway
in my thirties how long can I carry on doing this, and who
did I think was taken in by the trick to start with, I like to think
she meant that I didn't need all this; she knew about the trick.

Recreation

These are recurring meetings he mentioned, and before we began I remembered
that the last three times we'd tried this, I had wound up kicking off.
This I put down to recurrence itself, rather than anything said.
I've never been good at repeats, though to check my history, you could be
forgiven for thinking repeating my thing, particularly recitation
or any recreation of the better words of others.
Were *stop me if you've heard this before* to actually apply,
I'd barely trot a word out before you'd raised your hand.
There's a concentric layout to them when seen from above:
the repeated pleas to stop the recited stand-up shows of long ago
that are themselves rehashes of the artist's older stuff.
You wonder how many layers of ringfence one guy can maintain.
But if these were really recurring meetings, I'd know what was coming
I pointed out to the mirror that the camera had become.
He didn't say a word to this, but then he never does.

Blood

Listening to Scandinavian folk music played on the same instruments
that they'd have been a millennium back, I catch myself trying to hear
whether a drumskin splashed in the blood of the player
sounds different to one that isn't. I must stop reading interviews with musicians,
as this is not the first time this kind of sneakthievery's occurred
and I've tried to slip my hand under a sound, lift it softly and find something
       more.
Much of this has got to be down to my father, as not only do I share his blood
but his calling and pay have been dependent on
effective transubstantiation – so far as such a thing exists –
for longer than I've been alive. That being said, all I've got on dad is from
the once that I summoned the calm to ask him if he believed in all of that
       holy-end shit,
about it literally becoming blood, and all he gave was
'What I would say is that after you've spoken the words,
the thing being offered is not what it was.'
In the arena of the unhelpfully wise, or at least those so by intention,
my father has long reigned supreme, and this answer that – as I recall –
I took so poorly it broke my calm as a drop will a bowl,
sums up their inclination well: to offer something to transform you into blind
       rage;
but the something, later, is not what it was, and somehow you have more.
The substance of value, as it is on the altar, is to do with what you find you've
       received.
Remember that Balder, god of beauty, was brought after all from a bowl of spit,
but I doubt people brought it up either with him and that damn face,
or when taking in for the first time that most beautiful person who's just
       walked in.
Mind, the given and taken sometimes spend themselves in the exchange.
I remember the spatter of nosebleed dripped onto her bare chest
as we turned together after two days spent on nothing but cheap white,
rollies, and lemon-cut coke: the engine room of the poetry world.
It was different from the careful, brush-like, smearing and striping
of my chest with your blood as I held one of your hands,

and you held the rest of me. For all that we gave and took from each other, you're still left wanting more; as I am now, leaning my ear, trying to pick out the sound of dried blood.

The Reading

ars phonetica

It isn't how she tells it, no;
a lot of thought has gone under that bridge
to turn an evening, years ago,
into a sharpened edge.

Something to do with her accent,
filling out the tale.
A MidAtlantic accident:
that *Well* within the *Whale*.

And though I knew something else
I'd no idiolect to correct her,
to find the *fall* that calls in *false*
nor the lyre that sings in liar.

The Devil's Tattoo

You've got to stop drinking. If I had a pound.
You've got to stop drinking. Like most of my stripe I've reddened the day
with examples of these hours and that day and half a week, years ago,
when I could take it or leave it, and I don't know why you carry on saying
You've got to stop drinking. You know the sad thing, that they never tell you,
is I don't actually drink that much – no, I know, that's just what I'd say, but
it's true. Watch. There are days I can make it all the way through,
go to bed confused with myself, with half a bottle of Grant's on the bookcase
in case I wake fast and need to get back. The thing that kicks me into whisky
and pours me out like so much wine are the flashes of the other world
that I cannot crawl away from. To not drink at the sight of the dog
dragged by its owner, or that of the child at the party in the next room
who – every time I walk past the door, to get another drink – I see
behind all the fun of the rest, terrified that they will ask him to join in?
And as your man said, it's true, the *poor shall be with you always,* and there's
ever been shite in the universe, but that's it, cannot you see that, really?
I'm thrilled that you can get through it. No, really, I'm impressed
that it doesn't slug itself into your guts and tip your stomach out your eyes.
Fair play to you. Well done. You really did stand behind me that day,
on the walk to the station through the woods. You followed my eyes
and thought that the guy storming off the path into the trees
was just going to do what you'd imagine, hands out of sight,
and that wasn't a scream that you heard. You walked on to the station,
calling for me every ten steps or so, as I watched the guy leave the bushes
and wipe the blood on his jeans, and pocket the mobile and savour the ribbon
before pushing past me and half-running home. You got the train
as I followed him in, used my right to begin, locked the door, got the knife.
Now you wonder why she left, and why they let me go
at a good time in the market. You sound the devil's tattoo
You've got to stop drinking and don't even notice
the tears in my eyes. Was the ride from Barnes
to Vauxhall so quiet, daughter, that you barely noticed
your old man gone, and anyway put it down to the drink?

The Invitation

The barbarians are rarely at the gate. They are usually living with you.
They will show you the invitation you sent, when you ask for it. Which you do.

The Revenant

New Year's Eve and there was me having said to Michael sure, no problem,
I can help behind the bar until ten; if there's a tab at the end.
All going well, and with Jem in with Jess and Carey and their guys
I'd neared the famed land of content by half eight. Hell has always been wise
        to me
and clearly picked up something like a smile each time I pulled a pint.
At nine, then, the black stuff coughed white, and I filled the bucket
before nodding to Mike that I'd be away downstairs for a sec
and could he deal with that lot at the end of the bar, who needed the chuck if
        they didn't stop?
Halfway to the cellar, I'd got the feeling that someone was watching
but sure doesn't Hell have eyes in all the dark places,
and what was going to happen – the feted last words of each fool at the foot
of a cliff or an overdraft, all spread out – really, what, in this wee trip?
The barrel changed, and the dials alright, I got myself out. Halfway up, face to
        jaw,
the frothing of spit and the bomber's drone, the heir to Wee Jamie – remember
        Wee Jamie,
who'd take your leg off as soon as bark? – and clearly set on outdoing his dad.
Midnight can go to Hell when it comes to the courage, or lack of courage,
        available
when dealing with a dog who is literally higher up the ladder
and is considering which part of you is likely to reward most the effort
of putting his teeth to work. Sitting amongst the barrels,
I started studying how I might compare the cellar around me–
no, I've made that mistake before. I noticed the dials on the cider drop,
and swapped old for new, since I was down here. Five minutes later, same
        with the Stella.
Twenty-five on, and my hammering unanswered, I fitted the John Smiths,
stuck two Smirnoff in the lift when it came, and then a box of white. By
quarter to twelve, I was king of the place. The airshaft up to the street
allowed me a funnel for the fags that I promised I'd pay back for later.
An Elmore Leonard perched on the fuse box really hooked me in the second
        chapter,

and do you really need more than a packet of crisps, when you've none but
        yourself
for company, and little but Jack to drink? At ten past one, the door started
        banging
and I let Mike into my home. 'I thought you'd fucked off – you been stuck
        down here?
Why didn't you call?' And then I burst 'I've been down here for four *fucking hours!*
Did you wonder the barrels were changing themselves on the busiest night of
        the year?
You've got to do something about that dog!' After a while, he straightened up,
though the laughter still fair streamed down his cheeks, and he got me up
to the almost-bare pub, where Jem, who reckoned she'd guessed what had
        happened
gave me the hour-late dance and the kiss. And just after three, as we shut up
        behind us,
we came out to once again behold the street, before wandering our soft way home
to what we knew would be an exercise of ambition over capacity.
So four hours is the allowance that it would seem those I love will let out,
with me on the end, into the places that do not include them,
before wondering where the fuck he's gone. Only four hours down below,
and it was comfortable enough.

After the Iron Age

With that way private school kids have, though,
he managed to get himself into the mindscape of the wronged party,
by way of my calm, and particularly fixed on the fact that I hadn't
replied to the pictures he'd sent me, after, with any of my own.
With the dark coming on and my second beer done with, I saw an out in
      telling the truth.
I wasn't going to keep yours, so why'd I have sent you mine?
This really pissed the Harrovian off, as the idea that I could get rid of him
seemed to be worse than anything he could have done to me,
and after a minute of his kind of shouting I saw that he really expected
an apology. Of all the things in the world, I thought of
the tip on the estate, with its single knackered scratching post, soaked, at the
      top of the pile.
People tear up at highchairs and pushchairs on that heap. Not me: the kid has
      surely
outgrown them and, when we buy the things so cheap, this is where they
      belong.
A cat, though, never stops needing a scratch, so when you see the post thrown
      out
it's a fair bet the creature's dead. I tried in my anger to tell him this.
I never keep pictures *she* sends me, because we are past that.
But I didn't keep his because I knew that we were dead. *I knew it that morning*
I wish I'd told him *when you fiddled with your wallet as I pulled on my clothes.*
Were we on the level, I'd have walked him to the tip,
but he was in a cab by then
and I was glad he'd got it.

Madman

In Memory of Audrey Parkin

There's a man gone mad, lost his mind tonight
— *Blood Brothers*

After having messed up a eulogy at my gran's memorial service
I started smoking more, in a way that she would have got.
The weather is dealing with higher things these days
as we dare it to flood or fire, but occasionally it returns to the normal demands
of the English climate, and so my four-fag sessions at night, repeated,
are chased away quickly, and constellations, that could give me something
more to set this conceit against, disappear into cloud and rain. Then again,
she would have hated my dealing with her death through the plough
or starry bears, or through any form of navigation that did not factor in
Andy Williams, Julie Andrews, or even Willy Russell, to whose *Blood Brothers*
she was introduced too late to include in the setlist of the Spennymoor Show.
What we'd have given to hear Kath Carr belt out *Tell Me It's Not True*
or *Marilyn Monroe*. Gran understood, though, more than anyone
that I've met, about the razor's edge balancing public from private,
the words we pass on and those that simply work ourselves.
She was the Roy Keane of below-table-communication
and I'm fairly sure certain dints in my shins to this day can be traced
to her wanting me quiet. *The value of the marketplace is different to that
of the bedside table,* is how this translates to me,
though I know that she'd never have said it.
The impasse reached with this knot of thwarted grief stuck in my mouth,
I address my nightly uncertainty to Jon Hamm as Don Draper; a performance
        that,
again, arrived too late to give her something to see, something she'd have liked.
I bought her the first series about eighteen months before
my aunt and me mam decided that she could no longer face herself.
I'd been told episodes and timelines help people with what was gripping her,
and will grip me one day, and I pray will do so with such horror and might
that others of my blood be spared it.
Sure: I barter with sacrifice, in the face of the silent sky.
So aye, I'd hoped that Madison Avenue in the Sixties might have sorted it.

Guess what. It didn't. Now I seem to be on it myself as if to hope that,
rewatching it in my thirties, it might buy me a few years down the line
before we have that conversation again and I must move house.
When I first watched it, she was half herself, my grandfather having taken
half of her with him the night that he left,
and part of this is a form of reparation for not just moving back
up North back then and saving her from what none will be saved from
by, like Linda between Mickey and Eddie, *just being there.*
This time, though, I think I've got the dosage right,
the measure of the offering, as Draper rises into view. I watch,
the marriage failed, the promise gone, ability traded for cash and a sense
of the wider world having narrowed into not fucking stuff up,
or at least not fucking stuff up quite as often now.
Gran, you'd fucking love this show, and I miss not watching you watch it.
I'm sorry that I got all of this wrong. I'm sorry that this doesn't work.

The Iron Age

The only thing I can remember from Harrow is a story about a veteran physics
master who, according to legend, found a couple of boys doing something in his
house, and said, "I don't mind mutual masturbation, but I draw the line at buggery."
It was quoted from time to time as a bit of an accepted rule.

— *Francis Wheen*

I lie awake next to him, my eyes as shut as I can keep them,
and wait for the alarm that he'd told me about, as an afterthought, at four a.m.
The alarm goes off, and we both stay still. I can tell he's awake but
am fairly sure that this is a one-way thing. The noise continues
for close to a minute. I wonder what someone is waiting for.
If he thinks that I'm waking for his alarm, to either try again or leave,
then he really is everything that, the next week, I'll realise he is.
After that minute the alarm goes off in a different way, as he touches it.
I do some stirring, but more as a way of warning that I may soon wake up.

It was the first time since his first time that there'd been something new to try
and, while I'd experienced rituals like his before, it had been sweat
from me to keep the whole thing lit. The hours in the bar at least
had made clear he was trying new things. I'd asked if he knew the other meaning
that *trying* could have in that sentence, and the apology was laughter, contact,
and this time his arm didn't leave my wrist. Later, at the end of the bed,
which was also the start, he sat on the edge as naked as you
and gently reached his shaking touch to my thigh as I undressed, stood
between his knees. He looked up seeking a permission that I couldn't give.

Immediately afterwards, again that boy sat nervously on the end of his bed,
he toyed with the sports bra, felt the zip at its centre, and the same with my skirt.
I realised the sense of the words of God in *making all things new*, but felt
that however atheistic his bookshelves might appear, God would still get down
        his spine
if I brought it up right then. To see him there, though, sitting again
at the end of his own bed, which I knew, from the bedside table,
was usually an effective machine, I felt the scare of the sudden new:
it was not the first time he'd handled a bra, but it was the first time like this;
not the first time a skirt had come off in his hands, but it was like this.

And that flawed, beautiful trying, when it came to matters most familiar.
I tried, as I had tried before, to magic it away from him, to place a void
between my legs that he could stare at all he liked but not see what was there.
He could kid himself about smooth legs and recognise a nipple.
We could laugh about smears of makeup on the insides of his thighs
and where I would let him go, *that two out of three isn't bad*. He had coughed.
But he brought the full weight of his life before then to what he touched by
        chance
and there was no getting away from the sense that this was now
the first bronze shield shattered by the sudden iron, and the shock across his
        face.

So I stir and roll over and look, and he tries on four masks in twelve seconds.
Somebody smiles at me, laughs at the time, gives the top of my head a kiss,
goes to turn the filter coffee machine on, dressing as he does.
The private school kid talks to me about the day ahead, how busy the week
will be, but don't worry, he'll call me once stuff's straight again.
The boy from last night reaches over to me, feels the skin across my chest, he
kisses every scar, rolls me up in my own forgetting and holds me for an hour.
It is the stranger in the fourth that I stare at as I dress; who needs to wash last
        night from him,
and so really needs me gone. The stranger, from a separate place, already returned.

The Shipwright's Arms, Five p.m.

(after Arthur Rimbaud's 'At The Green Inn, Five in the Evening')

An hour of track, then mud and stream-burst.
Caked-up and flaking, I got down to Helford
and shouldered the door of The Shipwright's Arms,
tripped into the bar, ordered pint and short.
Shuffling around on the barstool, I adjusted my eyes
and dropped my ears into the swampy band
'Thanks....this is a shanty we've not tried before...
we don't know if it works.' The barmaid winces for me,

her top telling me the volume that she prefers, and its cut
swoops to murmur where that noise might lead.
She suggests a go, brushing my finger,
and I touch for a second, but know this to be a threshold
that I'm too tired to ease us over. We both move on.
I take half the pint in one, feel spring pour inside me.

The Trail

Lifting my right arm after I've dried myself
the stark flesh brought up sparkles, and not
a nick from the blade. I cannot help but notice, though,
that one old curve of raised white, arching in from my back.

Shaving raises all manner of dead in gone-at flesh below the hair,
but some still grab you. There are scars that we don't recall.
How can you not remember he'd laughed nervously that once
as I'd raised my arms above my head, after, and he'd seen it.

I think I was going at behind, my shoulder? With a longer blade, that time.
This reply did more to unsettle him than my silence had, before.
In fairness to him, there are scars on my back that I've never seen,
which were done by other people, and which I swallowed for years.

In front of the mirror now, though, I'm not sure if this is one of them,
or if I'd told the truth. The ones in front might as well be brands;
I mean, with some I could give you dates and times, knives, even whys.
But this wee lick, I'm not so sure. The other side's fine, I check.

I'd pulled him a little closer, as we'd slept, then. Happy that he'd got off.
The next morning, neither before nor after, he'd moaned *Maybe
it's the scar that time won't heal* in an odd choice of words
for what we were at as he said them. Still, it was poetry. It sealed.

And I'd not the words to tell him, then, as I think that I have now,
that *Scars* are *the healing of time, they just come with a receipt.*
Dressed as myself, after all these years, the scars are counterpoint
to the tighter jeans, the snugger top, the fuller chest, and these eyes.

He might just have had a point, mind, I reflected later, as in the shower
I inspected the mess of skin across my stomach. You see – or would,
if I let many more do so – there are marks, and there are markings.
There are the specific reliefs of horror, and then there are its wanderings

that speak more of wildernesses, white winds and a lack of shelter.
These definitive slits and ridges that I bare beneath the safer blade
are signatures of a type, that I never intended to heal like this
and expected to carry in shame from the moment that they got in.

The messes on my back from others, or those that I don't remember;
they're the blank sites in archaeology, too vague to be termed 'ritual'
but present nonetheless. The unwelcome mark, or unseen scar
at every heal. Something like that, which scares me more than him.

This evening I get in, undress and check again. That white smile
curling out from my armpit has set me off once more on the trail.
Lying in bed I feel it lead me past the last watchtowers, into woodland,
the stars scraping by up above, and the old sound of pain somewhere ahead.

Acknowledgments

My thanks to the editors of magazines and websites where several of these poems have previously appeared; Gerry Cambridge at *The Dark Horse*, Rob Selby at *Wild Court*, Fran Lock and Jack Varnell at Social Yet Distant, and likewise thanks to Kit Ingram and Aaron Kent at Broken Sleep Books.

Thank you to those who helped with the reading and work on these poems: Alison Brackenbury, James Brookes, John Challis, John Clegg, Matthew Griffiths, David Harsent, Kirsten Irving, Fran Lock, Richie McCaffery, Nicola Nathan, Abigail Parry, James Peake, Sam Quill, Yvonne Reddick, Declan Ryan, Rob Selby, Ali Siegenthaler, Richard Skinner, Alice St Clair, Jon Stone and Lewis Todd. Thanks also to my family.

The words do not yet exist to fully express my gratitude to and appreciation of Olivia Evans.

LAY OUT YOUR TRICKS

www.ingramcontent.com/pod-product-compliance
Lightning Source LLC
Chambersburg PA
CBHW021946040426
42448CB00008B/1262